SHIRE NATURAL HISTORY

THE
BARNACLE

CH00919031

MYRFYN OWEN

CONTENTS

Cover: *A barnacle goose (Branta leucopsis).*

Series editor: Jim Flegg.

Printed in Great Britain by C. I. Thomas & Sons (Haverfordwest) Ltd, Press Buildings, Merlins Bridge, Haverfordwest, Dyfed SA61 1XF.

Introduction

The barnacle goose *(Branta leucopsis)* is one of fifteen species of true geese in the world, all of them in the northern hemisphere. Geese are split into two types, grey geese *(Anser)* and black geese *(Branta)*. The barnacle is a small goose, weighing on average between 1.5 and 2.5 kg (3-5 pounds), with a grey body and a black neck. A conspicuous feature is the white or cream-coloured cheek patch; in several languages the barnacle goose has a name which translates as the 'white-cheeked goose'. It is very vocal; its call is a distinctive high-pitched bark like the yap of a small dog.

There are two other species of black geese native to Europe: the brent goose *(Branta bernicla)* is distinguished by being smaller than the barnacle, with short legs and a white rump which is particularly conspicuous in flight; the red-breasted goose *(Branta ruficollis)* is a small and very distinctive bird, with a russet chest and white barring on the flanks. The Canada goose *(Branta canadensis)*, a very large species, has been introduced to Europe and has a brown body and black neck.

Before man understood the migrations of birds, there was a commonly held belief in areas where barnacle geese wintered that the goose was associated with the barnacles that were found in the sea and were often washed ashore attached to pieces of wood (hence the name of the goose). The legend is described in Gerard's *Herbal*, first published in 1633.

Gerard reports: 'There are found in the North parts of Scotland and the Islands adjacent, called Orchades, certain trees whereon do grow certaine shells of a white colour tending to russet, wherein are contained little liuing creatures: which shells in time of maturitie do open, and out of them grow those little liuing things, which falling into the water do become fowles, which we call Barnakles; in the North of England, brant Geese; and in Lancashire, tree Geese: but the other that do fall vpon the land perish and come to nothing.'

He goes on to describe in detail the plumage of the barnacle goose and how the transformation takes place. He does, however, note that some 'Hollanders' report that they had seen the geese nesting in the Arctic. The legend did, no doubt, persist longer than it might otherwise have done because the geese were considered to be fish and could therefore be eaten by Catholics on Fridays.

There are traditionally three discrete populations of barnacle geese in the world, though a fourth, numbering up to five thousand individuals, has built up in Gotland and neighbouring islands in the Swedish Baltic. Breeding birds were first found there on the island of Laus Holmar in 1980. Their origin was unknown, but

Britannica Conchæ anatiferæ.
The breed of Barnacles.

1. *The barnacle tree, from Gerard's 'Herbal'.*

2. *Map of the breeding areas, migration routes and wintering areas of the three populations.*

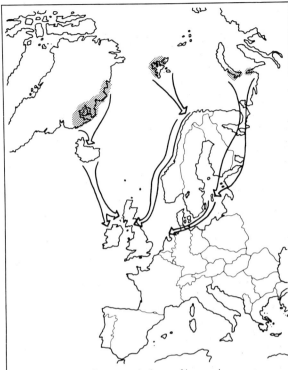

The three breeding populations of barnacle geese have quite separate wintering grounds. Even though the Greenland and Spitsbergen breeders winter within 100 miles of each other the two populations have rarely been known to intermix.

they probably originated from wild Siberian stock, perhaps following an injury of one of a pair when on spring migration in the Baltic, which is also a staging area for the Siberian breeders. The group grew quickly, to nearly five hundred pairs in 1985, and spread to nearby islands. The increase was probably helped by immigration of further Siberian geese coming there to moult and breeding in later years. The birds are nesting in this area when the wild stock is migrating through the Baltic on the way to their northerly breeding grounds. In the autumn, before the wild flocks have returned from the north, the Gotland geese fly south to the Netherlands to winter, and when the Siberian birds arrive in October the two groups intermingle. Since this Baltic population is rather different from the natural populations (it is probable that it could not have become established before man and his farm stock modified the vegetation on the islands), it will not be discussed further.

All populations are wholly migratory, breeding in the far north and wintering around the coasts of northern Europe, as shown in the map. Although the wintering areas of the three populations are very close (the Greenland and Svalbard breeders winter within 150 km, 100 miles, of each other), there is very little interchange between them. There has been a substantial amount of ringing of birds, especially in the Svalbard group. This has shown that only 0.1 per cent (one goose in every thousand) have emigrated to the other populations each year, and there has been no immigration.

By far the most important wintering area for the Greenland group is the island of Islay in the Inner Hebrides, where about two-thirds of the birds are found between October and March. The remainder of the population is scattered, mainly on islands, in other parts of northwest Scotland and in western Ireland. The Svalbard birds winter exclusively on the Solway Firth and those breeding in western Siberia are mainly found in Friesland and the islands off the north coast of the Netherlands, and in the Rhine/Maas delta near the Belgian border.

Barnacle geese are widely kept in captivity and the species bred in London Zoo as early as 1848. There are full-winged flocks in several of the centres of the Wildfowl and Wetlands Trust, the one at Slimbridge in Gloucestershire numbering more than two hundred individuals. These flocks are resident; geese always return to breed in the place where they were reared. A few birds may stray, but they have not established breeding flocks outside the protection of the enclosed areas. The single birds seen regularly in southern England mainly originate from captive stocks, although small flocks of Siberian breeders sometimes arrive on the east coast, especially during periods of severe weather on the European mainland.

Movements and ecology

Most animal migrations occur in response to changes in their food supply. Usually they capitalise on seasonal changes in food availability over a wide geographical range. In the case of most Arctic animals, the habitat is not available for them during a large part of the year. Barnacle geese are herbivorous throughout their life-cycle — geese are one of the very few vertebrate groups that nourish their young entirely on plant protein. Because their digestive systems are not very efficient, they must move seasonally to find the best feeding areas.

All three populations have developed remarkably similar patterns of movement. All breed between 70 and 80 degrees north and winter mainly between 50 and 55 degrees north in western Europe. Each population has a well defined spring staging area. The Greenland breeders leave western Scotland and Ireland in the last days of April and stop in the great valleys of northwest Iceland, before moving on to Greenland in mid to late May. The Siberian geese stay for a similar time in the islands of the Baltic, first Gotland and

3. *The movements of the Svalbard barnacle geese through the year, showing their location at all times. The blocks represent times when any geese are present; overlaps mean that some birds are at two or more locations.*

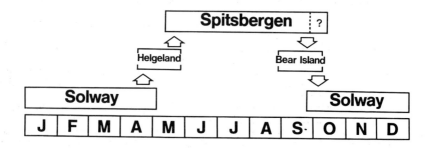

4. *A flock of geese on the staging islands in spring. The upturned boat in the background is used as an eider nesting hut.*

then the Estonian archipelago. On the return journey they probably fly most of the 3000 km (2000 mile) journey non-stop. The Greenland flocks have the shortest non-stop flight — they rest in southern Iceland to fatten up before the final leg of the flight.

The movements of the Svalbard geese, which probably have the most rigorous lifestyle of all, will serve to illustrate these journeys in more detail. The first birds arrive on the Solway wintering grounds between 20th and 30th September, exhausted from their long sea crossing. They encounter here the warmest temperatures of the whole of their life-cycles, as they take advantage of the relatively long days of October to regain their energy reserves in preparation for winter. During the winter they move only very short distances, using the area around Caerlaverock, south of Dumfries, the coastal flatlands 20 km (12 miles) to the west, and Rockcliffe Marsh, 20 km to the east. The Solway area experiences very little hard winter weather; there has not yet been recorded

a severe spell sufficient to cause the birds to move further south. The other populations similarly move rather short distances in winter; the Siberian birds redistribute themselves within the Netherlands, with more being in southerly parts in harsh weather.

Around 15th April the first flocks depart from the Solway for the spring staging area in Helgeland, just south of the Arctic Circle on the coast of Norway, about 1600 km (1000 miles) away. A few birds depart early, but most of the migration takes place over one or two days in the last week of April and the first week of May.

When the birds arrive in Norway, the temperature is just becoming warm enough for the grass to start growing on the treeless offshore islands on which the geese stop. The islands are flat, and the exposure and constant wash of spray preclude the growth of tall vegetation. The geese spend two or three weeks on the staging islands before travelling another 1600 km due north to the Svalbard archipelago, where they nest, mainly on small

5. *A family on the edge of a pond on Bear Island. The male (left) stands guard whilst his mate and three-month-old gosling (centre) feed.*

offshore islands off the main island, Spitsbergen.

The most southerly part of the breeding range is very far north, at about 77 degrees; when the geese arrive they may find the breeding area snow-covered. In very late seasons the geese may be unable to nest until mid or late June. There is little food available, so the birds remain inactive and survive on the energy reserves they have laid down further south.

The geese complete the breeding cycle in the short Arctic summer and they are on the way south again in September. Some flocks move about 300 km (180 miles) to the southernmost island in the archipelago, the bleak Bear Island, early in the month. These are mainly non-breeders; the young geese, still less than three months old, and their parents stay near to the breeding areas as long as possible, feeding on the lush vegetation on slopes fertilised by the large numbers of nesting seabirds.

Through the summer the birds experience no darkness but the nights are rapidly drawing in towards the end of September and, even if the ground remains snow-free, the geese have to move south. Usually, however, they are forced to go by the onset of winter — the first snowfalls can be as early as 15th September. Mass arrivals at Caerlaverock are very predictable in their timing — almost invariably between 20th September and 10th October.

In all their movements barnacle geese are extremely precise, and annual variations in dates are rarely greater than a few days. It is day length changes that determine their timetable, though winds are also very important. The geese fly at around 65 km/h (40 mph) in still air; clearly differences in wind direction and speed greatly alter the energy demands of such long-distance flights. Usually the birds wait for following winds and the absence of these may delay them for a few days. Normally in autumn the first blizzards come on strong northerly winds and these help to blow the geese south.

Unlike goose species that migrate overland, which can move slowly northwards as the snow clears, barnacle geese have no way of forecasting conditions on the staging and breeding areas. They therefore rely on moving at a fixed time when feeding conditions there are, on average, favourable. This means that in some years they will arrive too late and in others too early and this has an important effect on how well they breed.

The long-distance flights of geese are remarkable considering that they do not, like many seabirds and birds of prey, glide or soar — their wing loading is such that they have to keep flapping. We do not know accurately at what heights they normally fly, but they probably choose an altitude which gives them the greatest advantage from the wind. An airliner was struck by what was thought to be a goose when flying at over 10,000 metres (35,000 feet), and whooper swans have been reliably recorded at 8900 metres (29,000 feet). On the other hand, barnacle geese have been seen coming south into eastern Scotland very low over the waves when flying into the teeth of a gale.

The fact that the birds find their way with this precision over such huge distances is remarkable. Even when blown off course by a gale they usually manage to return to their normal range. Of 23 geese of the Svalbard population that strayed and wintered with flocks of Siberian barnacle geese in the Netherlands, seven returned to the Svalbard flock in subsequent years. The only goose of Greenland origin to be seen on the Solway (it was caught and ringed), spent one winter there and then dis-

appeared. It was recovered in Iceland, back in its native range, some years later.

This illustrates how traditional geese are in their range and timing: clearly this behaviour was evolved in a situation when it had large advantages for the birds' survival. In a landscape where suitable feeding and breeding areas were few and far between and only experience taught birds where to go, mistakes would have been very costly and the flocks moved over very strict routes, the young of the year migrating with their parents to traditional wintering grounds.

Let us consider how the barnacle goose may have fitted into the landscape of Europe before man and his grazing animals had had an impact on the native vegetation. When forests covered the lowlands of Europe there were very few areas of open ground where geese might feed. There were much larger expanses of estuarine land than there are today, but other species of geese like the brent were also competing for those habitats. With its short bill and rapid pecking action, the barnacle goose is adapted to grazing on very short swards. These were certainly to be found on the exposed offshore islands of Ireland and north-west Scotland. Here occurs a plant community known as a *Plantago* sward, which consists of very short salt-tolerant plants dominated by the sea plantain *(Plantago*

6. *A flock of wintering barnacle geese, unusually consorting with greylags (foreground) and a single pink-footed goose (far left).*

maritima). There are also a number of grass species, mainly red fescue *(Festuca rubra)*. *Plantago* swards have been described mainly from western Ireland, in areas where the barnacle goose still occurs. This may be the true traditional wintering habitat of the species. The barnacle goose also occurred on the west coast of England at least as far as Lancashire, according to the legend quoted earlier. Here it may have occupied saltmarshes, such as the one that exists today at Caerlaverock, or the short vegetation of dune slacks, those wet areas behind the coastal lines of sand dunes. The same may well be true of the flocks in continental Europe, and there the birds may also have exploited the vast areas of glasswort *(Salicornia)* beds which must have existed on the North Sea coast. The barnacle geese in the Netherlands still feed on the limited patches of this habitat that exist today.

Barnacle geese are still very largely coastal birds throughout the winter. The flocks normally roost on mud or sand flats and fly to feed on nearby saltmarshes or reclaimed pastureland. The feeding flights are rarely more than 5 km (3 miles) from the roost. They feed in large, tightly packed restless flocks, with small groups always in flight in search of a better feeding patch. This behaviour is very characteristic — the flocks are probably more concentrated than those of any other species of goose.

When the birds arrive on the wintering grounds, they are in rather poor condition after a long migration and need to lay down fat reserves which will carry them through any harsh winter weather which might make food hard to find. At this time they regularly eat a wide variety of seeds, a rich source of energy. Traditionally these would have been stripped from the standing stalks of grasses, sedges and rushes that are abundant on the saltmarshes, but more recently the flocks on the Solway have discovered that there are rich pickings on local barley stubble fields.

Later in the autumn, or when seeds are in short supply, the geese switch to grubbing out the stems of white clover *(Trifolium repens)* — stolons that run along the ground just above the soil level and which are abundant in most coastal swards where the geese feed. At the end of the growing season the clover plant draws all of the nutrients from the leaves into the stolons before becoming dormant for the winter. Stolons are a rich source of starch — indeed they taste much like peas! The birds' rather poor digestive system is illustrated by the fact that clover plants have been grown from pieces of stolon that have passed through a goose.

In midwinter the barnacle goose obtains most of its food by grazing, with a rapid pecking action. When the sward becomes very short the bird increases its peck rate, up to a maximum speed of more than two hundred pecks a minute. At this rate it can graze effectively on very short swards, less than 1 cm high. Even though it grazes so quickly, it is very selective about which plants or which parts of them it eats. There is a wide variety of plants on the saltmarsh (merse) on the Solway and the geese exploit them as each becomes most digestible. Each species of plant has its own growing characteristics, and the birds switch between them according to which provides the best nourishment (usually the one that is at its earliest stage of growth).

In the spring, as the grass comes to its first flush of growth and the days are lengthening, the geese begin to lay down fat and protein reserves in preparation for migration and breeding. The largest store of fat is held in the rear abdomen and, as they fatten, the geese become markedly more rotund in this area, a feature used as an indication of how well the birds are performing in a particular year. There are marked differences in body condition between years, depending mainly on the earliness of the spring.

Because the female is responsible not only for laying the clutch but also for incubation, she has to lay down greater reserves than the male, who spends much of his time in the spring protecting his mate from interference from other birds. The female increases her weight from about 1.6 kg (3½ pounds) during winter to as much as 2.5 kg (5½ pounds) — as heavy as the larger male — just before migration.

7. *Geese grazing on the staging islands in Norway at the end of May. Note the rounded profile of the abdomen, where fat is stored in preparation for the final stage of migration and for breeding, and the ringed bird on the right.*

By moving to the staging area in Norway the geese ensure that they capitalise on another spring. The fat that they use for the flight is replenished there — they actively feed for about eighteen hours per day during the staging period. On the staging islands the birds seem to have traditional feeding sites, places as small as a few yards in diameter, which are visited year after year. Different pairs even have different diets, and this may well reflect in their breeding success. Certainly those which are fattest on arrival on the breeding area have the best chance of sustaining themselves through the weeks when food is in short supply and the duties of incubation dictate different priorities, and of breeding successfully.

Man has reclaimed much of the traditional habitat of the barnacle goose and nowadays the majority of birds in all three populations are found on grasslands in winter — usually the heavily fertilised and improved swards where the most nutritious forage can be found. In some places the geese are deserting their traditional haunts in favour of these areas. The saltmarshes are deteriorating as farmers find it less profitable to graze valuable stock on these rather dangerous places. The same goes for offshore islands: fewer are now populated with sheep and cattle as the economics of farming on these marginal sites becomes more problematical.

On the new habitats there is little doubt that the geese do very well, but this is at the expense of the farmer. On the island of Islay in the Inner Hebrides 20-25,000 geese of the Greenland population, about two-thirds of the whole stock, spend the winter. Farmers on the island already have the disadvantages of having to bring in all stock feed by boat and to send their farm produce great distances to market. In this situation the geese are a final handicap. Their close grazing, well into the growing season, not only reduces the yield of spring grass but also, because the birds choose the most nutritious grasses, reduces the quality of the sward for farm stock. Although the barnacle goose is protected by European Community legislation, as a species which is scarce in world terms, licences have been granted to shoot it on Islay, in defence of the farmers' grass. The growth in the population in the 1970s was checked by the shooting and the number of geese in the Greenland stock remained relatively stable in the 1980s.

Social and family behaviour

In the long days of spring, when paired mature geese are laying down fat reserves in preparation for the breeding season, young birds search for mates. Most pair formation appears to happen without much fuss, but there are occasionally contests between males over females. The most obvious pairing behaviour is known as 'herding', where a male singles out a female from a flock and separates her from competing males by continually interposing himself between her and the rest of the flock. If there is competition, this behaviour can result in the males pursuing the female in a dash through the flock. These chases are always accompanied by loud calling and an aggressive 'wing-flicking' display where each wing is flicked upwards in turn while the bird barks loudly. Sometimes there are also aerial chases, usually involving two males and a female.

Whereas obvious pair-formation behaviour is seen mainly in spring, pair formation, surprisingly, seems to occur throughout the year. Studies of the Solway flock indicated that pairs formed equally in each season. Females endure more stress than males, which live longer, and this results in a surplus of males in the population. Unpaired mature males pair with young females in their second summer, and geese of between one and two years old pair through the following winter and spring.

Established pairs continually reinforce the pair bond with greeting and other displays. The most spectacular of these is the so-called *triumph ceremony*. The two members of the pair stand alongside each other, facing in opposite directions. They pump their heads up and down while calling loudly. This behaviour is most evident after the pair has been in conflict with another, the winning pair indulging in this self-congratulatory behaviour. Newly established pairs perform elaborate displays more frequently than do long-standing partners, as though they need continually to convince each other of their loyalty.

Geese are generally regarded as pairing for life, though evidence for this usually comes from the farmyard or from captivity, where there is little choice of potential partners. It is very difficult to collect information from the wild since convincing evidence of 'divorce' depends on knowing that both partners are still alive. This has been possible in the study of the Solway barnacle geese, where large numbers of birds have been individually marked for many years and are identifiable from a distance.

Rather surprisingly, an annual divorce rate of 2 per cent was found: that is, two out of every hundred pairs split up each year even though both partners remained alive. A closer study of the separations, however, showed that they normally occurred at the time of migration. If a bird lost its partner on the journey north and summered in a different area, it paired up very quickly, so that it stood the best chance possible of breeding in the next year. Each partner would be likely to pair up with a new mate as though its original partner was dead. There was even an example of a pair separating on spring migration, at least one partner being paired to a new bird in summer, and the original pair reuniting again when they relocated each other in the wintering grounds.

Such a strong bond must have powerful selective advantages. The reason for lifelong monogamy in geese is simply that long-established pairs breed better than new ones. If an individual loses its mate during the course of a winter, the chances of breeding successfully in the following summer are only a third of those of mates that stay together. This is because the division of labour between partners is essential to successful breeding. Barnacle geese breed in an unpredictable environment and perfect co-operation between mates is required to hatch eggs and rear young successfully.

A surprising but intriguing finding of these studies was that young birds reared in the same area paired preferentially

8. *Herding and other pair-formation behaviour. The male interposes himself between his selected female and competing males.*

with each other, although that pairing took place two or three years later. This is not merely because they occur in the same sub-flocks and are more likely to encounter one another; the population appears to mix thoroughly on the wintering grounds. It may be that in choosing a mate a goose is attracted to a specific trait, such as a dialect or a variation of behaviour that characterises its own area. This could be advantageous if both partners are adapted to the same environmental conditions.

As do other geese and swans, the barnacle goose has an extended period of family life; the parents care for the young for most of their first year. The family travels together to the wintering grounds and parental protection and help in food finding are beneficial to the survival of the young. In the early stages the male takes on the full responsibility for watching out for danger, but by midwinter both parents spend an equal amount of time being vigilant. Young geese within a family are able to spend long periods in uninterrupted feeding.

After the turn of the year, more and more young birds voluntarily leave the family and by the spring only a third of the goslings are with their parents. It is at this time that there is a conflict for the male's attention between guarding his mate and caring for his brood. The more stubborn offspring are eventually chased away by their father.

There are feeding advantages from being a member of a family. The larger a group of geese the more successful it is in contests with other groups: pairs beat single birds, families beat pairs and larger families overcome smaller ones. The result is that the largest families get the best food (they are always at the edge of the flock and gain first access to new grass) and presumably survive better.

Within a flock, there are always some birds on the look out for signs of danger. These are not altruistically acting as 'sentinels' on behalf of the others, but adults looking after themselves and their families. As the number of birds in a flock increases, the amount of time that each individual spends alert declines, so that there is an advantage to each individual to be part of the flock. There may also be feeding advantages of flocking: the easiest way for a bird to find a good source of food is to join a group which is already contentedly feeding.

9. *A barnacle goose on the nest, with the male standing by.*

10. *A sheltered nest site among the rocks. Note the copious down, plucked from the female's breast, and the droppings surrounding the nest, evidence of the female's feeding during incubation breaks.*

11. *Purple saxifrage — (Saxifraga oppositifolia), one of the food sources of the barnacle goose.*

12. *A family of barnacle geese.*

The breeding season

When a pair of barnacle geese arrives on the breeding grounds, the female is almost ready to lay her eggs. Any delay means that her body reserves will be used up and the chances of successful breeding in that season are in jeopardy.

Barnacle geese are too small to be able to defend their nests successfully against the Arctic fox, so they must find nesting sites which foxes cannot reach. In Greenland and in parts of Siberia and Svalbard the geese nest on cliff ledges, rising sheer sometimes 60 or 70 metres (200 feet) from the valley floor or from the sea. Most of the nests on Spitsbergen are on rocky offshore islands, shared with nesting eider ducks, skuas and glaucous gulls.

The female finds a sheltered spot, perhaps on the leeward side of a rock or on a ledge, to make the nest — in the long period of incubation she needs to minimise heat loss, so that she has to do the least possible amount of feeding, and stay as loyal as possible to the eggs. Because good sites are valuable, the same ones tend to be used year after year, probably by the same female. The female takes sole responsibility for the nest. Sitting on the tundra, she scratches the ground with her sharp claws to make a depression or 'scrape', where the eggs will be laid. There is little material available to line the nest, but what there is the female gathers while sitting in the depression or nearby and passing material over her shoulder into the scrape. Although barnacle geese nest in loose colonies, they are aggressive and territorial. The male jealously guards the area around the nest, keeping away other birds that threaten the female or the nest, and particularly prospecting pairs that might take over the nest site.

The eggs are creamy white and weigh about 100 grams (4 ounces) each; they are laid at near-daily intervals until the clutch, usually of three to five eggs, is complete. The last egg is usually slightly smaller then the rest. On the day before the last egg is laid, the female begins to incubate. Over the next week she plucks down from her breast so that there is a thick covering around the eggs. This down plucking has a dual function: it helps to insulate the eggs, and it exposes a bare area on the female's breast — the brood patch — which she keeps in contact with the eggs to heat them. She turns the eggs regularly, but, suspended in the albumen on spring-like coils, the embryo always floats to the surface and is always in contact with the brood patch. This is very important as the part of the egg in contact with the frozen ground will be several degrees cooler than that next to the female.

Incubation lasts for 24 or 25 days, during which time the male stands guard on nearby high ground. He is able to do some feeding while on duty or, if there is no vegetation near the nest, he takes short trips to nearby tundra. He is never out of earshot, though, and quickly returns when his mate calls.

When the female leaves the nest to drink, bathe and preen she carefully covers the eggs with down and the male stands guard over the nest. If both members of the pair leave together, the eggs are very likely to be predated by waiting skuas or gulls. On some nesting islands in Spitsbergen there is no food within reach and the birds have to survive entirely on their body reserves. The failure rate of nests is very high in such places, especially if the spring is late and the birds are not in their best condition. Where there is ample feeding on a nesting island or on nearby tundra, nearly all the nests will hatch successfully.

Where vegetation is sparse, the birds capitalise on a variety of food sources. Detailed studies by a Dutch team on Spitsbergen indicated how complex were the relationships between the geese and their food supplies. As snow clears from the tundra, new food sources are continually becoming available and females make use of several different food items. Among these are the flower buds of the purple saxifrage — the earliest plant to emerge from the frozen soil — willow buds and the tiny horsetail *Equisetum*.

13. *Rounding up a group of geese in Spitsbergen; the birds are driven from the pond into a net corral erected on the bank.*

Later, grasses and sedges begin to come into leaf. In the early days, when food patches were small, the researchers discovered that only the first female to find a new patch did well and that this had an effect on their breeding success. The best feeders, perhaps the most experienced, had a very high success rate and the same birds tended to be successful in different years.

In the last few days of incubation the goslings begin to peep within the eggs; this ensures that the whole brood hatches together. Both parents sense their imminent emergence; the female stays constantly on the nest and the male moves closer in. Almost as soon as the last hatched gosling is dry, the family leaves the nest and heads for the rearing areas on nearby tundra. The young hatch with a good reserve of food in the yolk sac — they may have to survive for two or three days without feeding.

The first journey is extremely hazardous for the young goslings. For cliff nesters, the initial fall of up to 60 metres (200 feet) is not dangerous in itself — the young are very light and do not damage themselves on the rocks below — but the foxes and gulls wait below the cliffs for any young that do not quickly relocate their parents. For island nesters, there may be a journey of up to 2 km (1¼ miles) to the mainland, with gulls ever on the watch for any young that lag behind.

Once on the rearing areas, the goslings grow quickly on the flush of vegetation high in protein. It is essential that the geese nest as early as possible so that the hatch is close to the start of vegetation growth. Because the female has almost fasted through incubation, she emerges in very poor condition and the male takes full responsibility for guard duties, whilst the female and her brood feed for up to 20 hours in every 24 in the continuous daylight of the Arctic summer. The families gather in loose aggregations so that the males can benefit from each other's vigilance.

Once the young have survived the first week, they have a very good chance of growing to the flying stage, which is only six weeks from hatching. The families run between lake margins as a group and only an occasional gosling is picked off by a

15

14. *The staging areas of Bear Island, with geese in the air.*

fox. The families usually move between a number of lakes or riverside pastures, cropping the vegetation on one before moving on. After the grass has rested, they return again to graze the new growth. By continually harvesting the vegetation, they ensure that it is kept in a young and palatable state — much higher in protein than are ungrazed plants.

It is in this time of continuous day length that the full-grown geese moult their primary flight feathers simultaneously and become flightless for about four weeks. The non-breeding birds, which are mainly immatures, have gathered on the coast, on the larger islands or around lowland pools while the

breeding pairs are nesting and they moult two or three weeks earlier than the breeders. These flocks are joined by any pairs that lose their eggs or young. They remain relatively inactive, feeding in the immediate vicinity of water and always keeping a watchful eye for marauding foxes. They do use up some of their body reserves, but the time of the moult is not a very stressful time for non-breeders.

By the time the goslings have hatched lakes at higher altitudes have cleared of ice and the families walk to these and generally do not mingle with the large flocks of non-breeders. The females lose their feathers as soon as they can, but the male parents, because of their important guarding role, delay their moult until the

15. *Flightless geese and goslings in a pen after being caught for ringing.*

16. *A flightless goose in the hand, showing the engraved plastic ring used for long-distance identification of individuals.*

young are about three weeks of age. The gander will fly to head off predatory gulls or mob marauding foxes while his charges reach the relative safety of the water. At three weeks of age, not only can the goslings run very quickly but they are too large for gulls to swallow, and the male himself becomes flightless.

By the end of July the non-breeders are again on the wing; as soon as they can fly, they gather on fertile patches of tundra, around lakes too far from the sea to moult, or at higher altitudes where plant growth is delayed, to begin fattening for the journey south. The best feeding patches are under the slopes or cliffs where seabirds breed. On Spitsbergen the tundra near colonies of little auks is very lush. The water from melting snow on the hills behind the moraines where the auks breed trickles down through the colonies and provides a liquid fertiliser for the otherwise barren tundra. In Greenland the large valleys are so fertile that rich vegetation grows without such help. Only when the birds are forced by their flightlessness to remain close to water is their food supply restricted.

The geese share their summer range with other birds and some grazing mammals. In Spitsbergen the land fauna is impoverished; the only mammals are the foxes and the short-legged reindeer. Elsewhere, musk-oxen, Arctic hares and lemmings take advantage of the tundra vegetation. In the short summer there is a profusion of flowering plants — small but none the less beautiful for that.

Other species of geese also share the tundra; in Greenland great flocks of pink-footed geese *(Anser brachyrhynchus)* fly from their breeding grounds in Iceland to moult in the valleys of Greenland with the barnacles. The pink-feet are larger than the barnacles and have a longer fledging period. This means that they cannot nest as far north, but they do exploit these northerly areas for moulting. During the flightless period there may be competition for the limited food supplies around suitable moulting lakes; the flocks of the two species tend to keep apart.

Pink-feet also breed on Spitsbergen, but they tend to occupy the large fertile valleys. The larger species can defend itself against the Arctic fox, and pink-feet are not restricted to islands or cliffs for nesting. Provided the site is easily defended from a fox, on an outcrop of rock or a steep slope, these geese can breed on the open tundra.

Brent geese also breed in Svalbard; these are birds of the light-bellied race that winter in Denmark and northern England. They used to occupy the west coast islands on which the barnacles now breed but, as the brent goose population declined following the great crash in their *Zostera* food supplies in the 1930s, they retreated eastwards and now breed mostly on a large number of tiny islands in the south-east. There is some debate whether the barnacles displaced the brent as their population increased or whether they merely filled the vacant habitat. We will never know, but surely the brent could not return to the west coast again if their population increased. An interesting situation is developing in the Tusenoyane, the remaining stronghold of the brent, where barnacles are now beginning to colonise. Will these chase away the smaller species? Since the brent is able to breed in a summer shorter even than the barnacle goose, it will probably still cling on in the most demanding places, close to the pack-ice that is present even in summer in the northern and eastern parts of Svalbard.

Little is known of the late summer movements of the barnacle geese nesting in Greenland or Siberia; they may well have gathering areas in the southern parts of the breeding range where they spend the last few days of summer. It was not until 1980 that it was discovered that the barnacle geese nesting in Svalbard used Bear Island, the southernmost island in the archipelago, as a final staging post before making the long over-sea crossing.

Bear Island is extremely exposed and often foggy, so the vegetation grows to only a few centimetres in height even though there are no grazing animals to exploit it. The geese arrive there in September and stay until the snow or shortening days drive them south. Again they are dependent on nutrients brought in from the sea — the most lush vegetation is found on seabird slopes or on headlands which serve as roosts for gulls.

Population dynamics

In the absence of immigration and emigration, which are not important in any of the groups of barnacle geese, the size of a population depends only on changes in the number of births and deaths. This chapter examines how the environment and attributes of the birds themselves govern the population changes over the years. Other aspects of population dynamics have been studied mainly through ringing, especially in recent years when coded rings readable at a distance have come into use.

Geese are long-lived birds and have an extended period of immaturity. Young birds pair in their second year of life, and some breed in their second summer. Certainly in captivity and in the early years of the Gotland population most two-year-olds do nest. In the harsher realities of the Arctic, however, only a few two-year-olds manage to rear young, and these are often paired to older mates. In the Svalbard population, nowadays, when numbers are high and there is much competition for nesting spaces and food during laying, very few geese breed successfully until they are three years old. Young geese are not as productive as adults until they are five or six years of age.

As shown in the previous chapter, the amount of body reserves that the female has when she reaches the breeding grounds is crucial to her success. The absolute limit is set by the amount of weight she can put on and still fly. We do not know how much this is, but in most years it is likely that the majority of birds do not reach their peak condition before the increasing day length tells them that they have to depart. From information on the profile of the abdomen of geese in the field, it seems that in most years the birds in the Svalbard population are heaviest when they leave the Solway; only in the most favourable springs are they able to make up the 160 grams (6 ounces) of fat that they use on the journey to Helgeland. The other populations have much shorter journeys to their staging posts and are at their heaviest just before departure to the Arctic.

The female has first to allocate part of her reserves to eggs, whilst leaving sufficient to sustain her through incubation. If the spring is delayed, the number of eggs in a clutch is reduced, and some of the leaner females may have to desert their eggs to feed. Others may not have sufficient reserves even to attempt to nest. It is the failure to nest and remain loyal to the nest until hatching that is responsible for the greatest loss of breeding potential in barnacle geese. For example, in Spitsbergen in 1986 each hundred mature females, if they had all laid and hatched their young successfully, would have raised 400 goslings. In the event, although the summer was favourable for breeding, only 160 eggs were laid per hundred females and about 80 young hatched, only a fifth of the potential.

The condition of the male is also important to the success of the nest since he must guard it against predation throughout incubation. On one island in Spitsbergen the success rate of nests in mossy habitat where males could feed close to the nest was considerably greater than that of those on rock or gravel.

Losses of goslings in the first week are another important factor limiting recruitment of young. In cliff nesters and those which have to make a long sea crossing from offshore islands, a quarter or more of the goslings succumb to predation. A further few are taken during the rearing period and, by the time the goslings fly, the average size of the broods on arrival at the wintering grounds is reduced from 3.5 to 4 at hatching to just over two.

This is not the end of the losses of goslings — the journey southwards is a hazardous one, and some of the late-hatched broods may have difficulty in gaining enough weight in the remaining part of the summer to provide them with sufficient energy. The Svalbard and Siberian breeders make the longest journeys; information on losses is available only from the former. In some years the passage of the marked parents and their

17. *Geese at the wintering grounds.*

18. *Geese on the traditional merseland (saltmarsh) habitat at Caerlaverock.*

young was monitored at Bear Island. In other years four- or five-week-old goslings were marked and checks were made as to whether or not they arrived safely on the wintering grounds.

Losses varied in different years, depending on the number of young being reared and the earliness of the winter. In years when there were few birds and good autumn conditions, only 10-15 per cent of the young died on the journey, whereas in the worst year, 1986, the losses amounted to 35 per cent. In that year it was clear that those goslings that hatched at the end of June stood the best chance of survival — about 80 per cent of those were seen in Scotland compared with only half of those that hatched in mid July. The best survivors, even within an age group, were also the heaviest. There is probably competition between the families for the best feeding areas on the tundra and, when there are many young, those with the least aggressive parents grow more slowly than those in larger dominant families. Not surprisingly, in view of this, geese that were reared in parts of the range with good vegetation did best.

Once the young have reached the wintering grounds, their survival is very high — in most years it is no different from that of adults. Their survival over the second year, before the birds are exposed to the stresses of breeding, exceeds that of older geese. Once young barnacle geese have reached Caerlaverock, more than four out of every five of them live to become two-year-olds and have a chance of breeding.

There are only three factors, predation, starvation and disease, which cause the death of birds, since there is no evidence that most geese reach what we would recognise as old age (though the aging process might lead to death from one of the other causes in the natural environment). Disease is uncommon among wild geese, unless they are subject to an occasional epidemic of afflictions such as duck virus enteritis, or duck plague, which is very rare in Europe. Among the many deaths that have been recorded in the Svalbard geese, only one was diseased, a female which died of avian tuberculosis.

Starvation is also unknown in modern times, when winter food supplies are, to all intents and purposes, unlimited. In earlier decades, when suitable wintering habitats were very limited, starvation must have been a common cause of death, especially in harsh weather. There are reports from the Outer Hebrides of emaciated birds being found in severe winters. There have been records of females of some goose species dying by starving themselves rather than desert the nest, but such deaths are rare and have never been recorded in barnacle geese. The only mortality recorded nowadays from causes related to starvation is of birds which cannot complete the autumn migration successfully. These presumably become exhausted and alight on the sea or on terrain where there is no food and subsequently starve to death.

Predation of adults on the breeding grounds is very low. The foxes are a constant danger, but they generally take goslings, which cannot run as fast as their parents. Moulting flocks of non-breeders are generally large and wary; they detect a fox long before it is in a position to pose any threat to them. The flightless flocks also use other birds to warn them of danger. Gulls and terns are extremely noisy when danger looms. A flock of geese has been seen to take to the water instantly when nesting Arctic terns began screaming and mobbing an approaching fox, even though that animal was well out of sight of the geese.

Predation by man is still usually the most important cause of mortality in goose flocks, although barnacle geese are protected by law from shooting throughout their range. On the Solway, shooting still causes the deaths of a few hundred geese each year. Much of this is deliberate, but sometimes barnacles are shot in mistake for pink-feet or greylags, which are legitimate quarry and which winter in the same area.

The Greenland birds on Islay, as mentioned previously, are shot in defence of farmers' crops. In the mid 1970s they were causing severe damage, when numbers of geese on the island rose to as many as 24,000 in one winter. A limited shooting season was allowed in the late 1970s and geese are still shot legally under licence from the Department of Agriculture and Fisheries for Scotland. In the late 1970s the kill was increased from 500-700 up to 2000 per year and this had an immediate effect on the size of the population, which declined to only 14,000 in 1982-3. Numbers subsequently recovered following the protection of the main feeding areas and a reduction in the adult mortality rate. The Siberian population is fully protected, most of its wintering areas are safeguarded and its adult mortality rate is the lowest of the three groups, at only 9 per cent per year from all causes.

Finally, let us consider the lifespan and expectation of breeding for individual geese that have been watched over a period of years, again taking the example from the Solway flock. The most complete information comes from a group of eighty geese marked as yearlings in Spitsbergen in 1973 (they were hatched in 1972). There was a considerable difference in survival between the sexes: the average lifespan of a male was ten years compared to the female's eight. This was expected because of the greater stresses on the female associated with laying and incubation, manifest probably in greater losses on autumn migration. Since the number of young a bird produces in its life depended largely on how long it lived, males also bred better than females.

The number of young reared by each individual was small, despite their long lives. About half the females and a third of the males died without breeding successfully, and only one, a male, reared more than ten young in its life. Despite the low breeding success, because adult survival was high the population as a whole grew during the period when these birds were alive. Overall, each pair produced more than the two birds required to replace themselves for the next generation.

As we have seen, the weather in spring and early summer is the main factor determining whether the population breeds well. How well an individual bird does during its life depends on the particular set of conditions it encounters. On average, birds living through the best run of years there were between 1970 and 1988 produced 40 per cent more young than those birds which lived through the leanest years.

The weather, as it affects the food supplies for fattening in the spring and in its effect on laying date and subsequent hatching success, is the most important factor determining how many young geese will be reared in any year. Man's predation continues to take its toll of adults but, in protected populations, competition for food and losses on autumn migration are likely to take over as the main causes of death. The popula-

19. *Graph of the growth of the Svalbard population and the reasons for its success.*

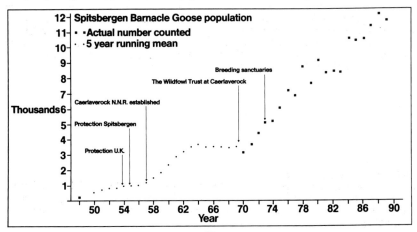

22

tion will stabilise when births and deaths balance each other; this stage seems to be approaching in all three populations, even for the new group of barnacle geese that breed in Gotland.

Conservation

The case of the barnacle goose as a species represents a success story for conservation. In 1959 the world population numbered a mere 30,000 geese, with nearly 20,000 of those in the Siberian population. The Greenland stock numbered only 8000 and there were no more than 1800 Svalbard breeders on the Solway. The species was protected in the Netherlands in 1946, following persecution during the Second World War, and the Siberian stock had increased considerably by the 1959 count. There was still a two month (December and January) open season on the birds wintering in Scotland outside the Solway, but the Spitsbergen stock became completely protected in Britain in 1954 and in Svalbard in 1955. The shooting season on Islay was terminated in 1981 when the Wildlife and Countryside Act became law; the only shooting allowed nowadays is under licence to prevent damage.

The case of the Svalbard barnacle goose, shown in figure 19, illustrates well the way in which increased protection from shooting has been reflected in the recovery of numbers. There were up to 6000 geese reported from the Solway in about 1900 and, whereas there is some doubt whether these were all of Svalbard stock, there is no doubt that numbers declined drastically in the early decades of the twentieth century and especially through the Second World War, when there were tank ranges on their main feeding grounds at Caerlaverock. The lowest point was probably reached in 1948, when no more than 300 birds were seen on the Solway. Numbers increased slightly in the following years, and the increase continued after protection in 1954. It was not until 1957, however, when a National Nature Reserve was established at Caerlaverock, that numbers began to increase sharply; the reserve protected a feeding area and provided a refuge from illegal shooting. In the 1960s the population seemed to have stabilised at 3000 to 4000 birds. In 1970 the (then) Wildfowl Trust took over land at Caerlaverock and increased the refuge area, and this prompted another sharp increase in numbers, to the present high level of around 12,000 birds. There seems now to be a depression of breeding and increased mortality caused by the large numbers, and the population is unlikely to grow much more.

What is likely to be the fate of the species in future? There is no doubt that all three stocks are now secure; all are protected from shooting and most of the wintering areas are effective reserves. The latest figures suggest that there are more than 120,000 barnacle geese in the world. There is a deterioration in some of the island habitats due to the withdrawal of farm stock from some of the remoter areas in Scotland, Ireland and Norway. This is not, however, having a decisive effect and management improvements which are being investigated might bring about a reversal. We can safely say, then, that this interesting species is safeguarded for the future.

ACKNOWLEDGEMENTS
Illustrations are acknowledged to: Joe Blossom, cover, 12; Chris Knights, 9; Owen and Gullestad (1984), 3; *Wild Geese of the World* (Batsford, 1980), 2, 8. All other illustrations are by the author and are reproduced by courtesy of the Wildfowl and Wetlands Trust.

Places to visit

The Wildfowl and Wetlands Trust has the aims of conservation, research, education and recreation, specialising in wildfowl and their wetland habitats. The Trust has nine centres throughout the UK and others are under development. All are open to the public (Llanelli from spring 1991) and seven have collections of tame wildfowl which can be studied at close quarters. The refuge at Caerlaverock has no tame birds but between September and April flocks of wild Svalbard barnacle geese can be seen there; at times the whole population resides on the refuge. Those wishing to learn more about wildfowl and wetlands are recommended to become members of the Trust; write to the Wildfowl and Wetlands Trust, Slimbridge, Gloucester GL2 7BT.

The centres of the Wildfowl and Wetlands Trust are at:

Arundel: Mill Road, Arundel, West Sussex BN18 9PB. Telephone: 0903 883355.
Caerlaverock: Eastpark Farm, Caerlaverock, Dumfries DG1 4RS. Telephone: 038777 200.
Castle Espie: 78 Ballydrain Road, Comber, Newtownards, Co Down BT23 6EA.
Llanelli: Penclacwydd, Llwynhendy, Llanelli, Dyfed SA14 9SH. Telephone: 0554 741087.
Martin Mere: Martin Mere, Burscough, Ormskirk, Lancashire L40 0TA. Telephone: 0704 895181.
Peakirk: Peakirk, Peterborough, Cambridgeshire PE6 7NP. Telephone: 0733 252271.
Slimbridge: Slimbridge, Gloucester GL2 7BT. Telephone: 0453 890333.
Washington: District 15, Washington, Tyne and Wear NE38 8LE. Telephone: 091-416 5454.
Welney: Pintail House, Hundredfoot Bank, Welney, Wisbech, Cambridgeshire PE14 9TN. Telephone: 0353 860711.

Further reading

Boyd, H. 'The Number of Barnacle Geese in Europe, 1959-60', *Wildfowl Trust Annual Report* ,12 (1961), 116-24.
Larsson, K.; Forslund, P.; Gustafsson, L.; and Ebbinge, B. S. 'From the High Arctic to the Baltic: the Successful Establishment of a Barnacle Goose *Branta leucopsis* Population on Gotland, Sweden', *Ornis Scandinavica*, 19 (1988), 182-9.
Ogilvie, M. A. *Wild Geese.* T. and A. D. Poyser, 1978.
Ogilvie, M. A. 'The Numbers of Greenland Barnacle Geese in Britain and Ireland', *Wildfowl*, 34 (1983), 77-88.
Owen, M. *Wildfowl of Europe.* Macmillan, 1977.
Owen, M. *Wild Geese of the World.* Batsford, 1980.
Owen, M., and Black, J. M. 'Factors Affecting the Survival of Barnacle Geese on Migration from the Breeding Grounds', *Journal of Animal Ecology,* 58 (1989).
Owen, M., and Black, J. M. 'The Barnacle Goose', in I. Newton (editor), *Lifetime Reproduction in Birds.* Blackwells Scientific Publications, 1989.
Owen, M., and Norderhaug, M. 'Population Dynamics of Barnacle Geese *Branta leucopsis* Breeding in Svalbard, 1948-1976', *Ornis Scandinavica* 8 (1977), 161-74.
Prop, J.; van Eerden, M. R.; and Drent, R. H. 'Reproductive Success of the Barnacle Goose *Branta leucopsis* in Relation to Food Exploitation on the Breeding Grounds, Western Spitsbergen', *Norsk Polarinstitutt Skrifter* 181 (1984), 87-117.